RC 182 R4

Everything You Need to Know About **Rheumatic Fever**

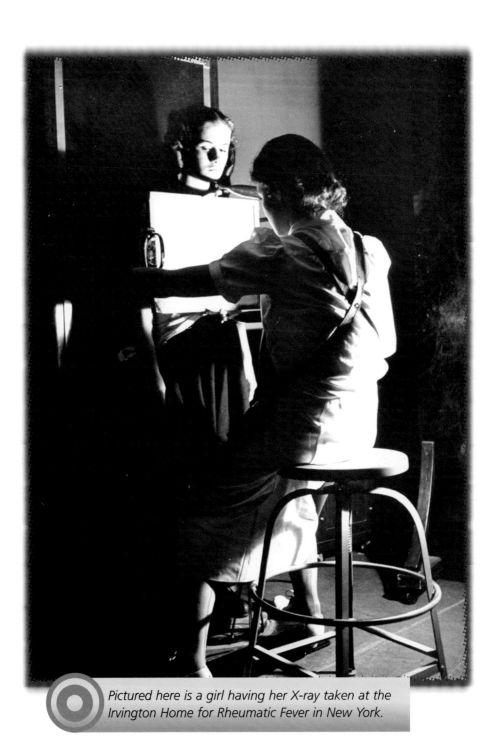

Pictured here is a girl having her X-ray taken at the Irvington Home for Rheumatic Fever in New York.

Everything You Need to Know About *Rheumatic Fever*

Phillip Margulies

The Rosen Publishing Group, Inc.
New York

Published in 2004 by The Rosen Publishing Group, Inc.
29 East 21st Street, New York, NY 10010

Library of Congress Cataloging-in-Publication Data

Margulies, Phillip.
Everything you need to know about rheumatic fever / by Phillip
Margulies.
        p. cm. — (The need to know library)
Summary: Presents an overview of rheumatic fever that includes the
history of the disease, new developments in combating it, and new
ways to prevent its spread.
Includes bibliographical references and index.
ISBN 0-8239-4509-X (libr. bdg.)
1. Rheumatic fever—Juvenile literature. [1. Rheumatic fever. 2. Diseases.]
I. Title. II. Series.
RC182.R4M28 2004
618.92'991—dc21
                                                            2003007164

Manufactured in the United States of America

Contents

Introduction

In the late 1980s, public health officials around the United States began to notice a disturbing trend. Patients around the country were showing up in hospitals with an illness that, until recently, American doctors had thought was beaten: rheumatic fever.

The reports came in from states as far apart as Utah, Ohio, California, Texas, Colorado, and Pennsylvania. In 1986 and 1987, ten recruits at the Naval Training Center in San Diego became ill. Between 1985 and 1987, the Primary Children's Medical Center in Salt Lake City saw more than 120 children with rheumatic fever. In 1986, doctors at the Children's Medical Center in Akron, Ohio, saw twenty-three cases of rheumatic fever—the decade before that, they'd seen only an average of two

Strep throat is an illness common among children that is usually harmless. But it can lead to rheumatic fever.

or three cases a year. In Columbus, Ohio, doctors saw forty cases in two years, more than they'd seen during the ten previous years combined. There were similar outbreaks in Dallas, Denver, and Pittsburgh.

Rheumatic fever, a disease that people often get a few weeks after they recover from a strep throat infection, is just what its name implies: a fever, or an abnormally high body temperature. But the fever is the least dangerous of its symptoms. The other symptoms of the disease are quite dangerous because they injure many vital parts of the body. Body joints may swell painfully, and the nervous system can be temporarily damaged, causing facial muscles to move at random. While these symptoms are uncomfortable and frightening, rheumatic fever has its worst and most long-lasting effects on the heart, making it the leading cause of heart disease among people under the age of fifty.

Rheumatic fever kills only some of its victims but leaves others weak and sickly for the duration of their lives. For nearly two centuries after it was first discovered, the fever was a major disease of childhood. Its victims filled hospitals and held parents in a grip of terror. But then, from the 1950s until today in the United States and Europe, the number of cases that occurred each year declined dramatically.

No one knows for sure why fewer people in the United States and Europe have been getting rheumatic fever today than in the past, but there are several possible explanations. Medicines such as antibiotics have become more effective at killing the bacteria that can lead to rheumatic fever. Also, people's overall living conditions have improved over the years. One especially interesting explanation, which we'll discuss more in the coming chapters, is that the bacteria that cause rheumatic fever may have changed.

Regardless of the reason, physicians are happy that the fever has become less common. The trouble is that when the number of cases begins to rise, as they did in the late 1980s, no one can be sure of the cause or how serious the problem might become. Luckily, while there were more cases of rheumatic fever in the late 1980s than there had been a few years earlier, the disease did not return to anything near its former numbers. Scientists today continue to research the illness to make sure it never reaches those numbers again.

Chapter 1

What Is Rheumatic Fever?

Rheumatic fever is a serious illness that can occur as a result of another illness that is usually minor. The minor illness is an infection called strep throat. The name strep throat is short for streptococcal pharyngitis, and the bacterium that causes it is called group A streptococcus (GAS).

While strep throat itself can be painful, it isn't considered a serious illness. Most people who get it recover with treatment, and sometimes even without treatment. Unfortunately, a few of those who recover get rheumatic fever, a serious disease that can cause long-term damage to the heart.

Some people with an intense form of strep throat also get a red rash that can appear in the form of tiny red bumps on the chest or abdomen. This form of strep throat is called scarlet fever and can also lead to rheumatic fever. Scarlet fever was once a very dangerous disease, but today it can be treated fairly easily.

At other times the strep bacteria infect the tonsils, a pair of glands located on each side of the throat. When this happens, the tonsils become swollen and inflamed, a condition called tonsillitis. Not all cases of tonsillitis are caused by bacteria—some are caused by viruses—but those that are caused by bacteria can lead to rheumatic fever.

Bacteria: A Closer Look

Bacteria are one-celled organisms, which are so small they can be seen only under a powerful microscope. They are the oldest forms of life on Earth—scientists believe that bacteria have been around for 3.5 billion years.

Many bacteria are harmless and many are useful. In fact, life on Earth couldn't go on without bacteria since they break down decaying matter and turn it into the soil that allows plants to grow. Bacteria that live inside our intestines help us digest our food. Bacteria help cows digest grass. Other kinds of bacteria turn milk to yogurt. Our lives benefit from these kinds of bacteria. Still, some bacteria can cause disease when they get inside our bodies and start multiplying.

One bacterium by itself can't affect a person very much, but bacteria are powerful in numbers and they reproduce very quickly. It doesn't take long for a few bacteria to become many. Every twenty minutes each bacterium splits and becomes two bacteria. Two become four, four become eight, and in a matter of days there are billions.

Bacteria also evolve to fit their environment. Because they produce a new generation every twenty minutes, we don't have to wait millions of years to watch bacteria evolve, as we have to with plants and animals. Bacterial evolution happens within decades or less. This means that the antibiotics we use today might not work several years from now because the bacteria have changed. In other words, the bacteria might have evolved into a form that is resistant to the antibiotics.

Today, many scientists and doctors worry about evolving strains of bacteria and, consequently, evolving strains of rheumatic fever. Bacteria are appearing that can't be killed by present-day antibiotics. Doctors are also seeing bacteria appear that cause new diseases and new symptoms in a never-ending battle.

Who Gets Rheumatic Fever?

Less than 0.3 percent, or three out of every 1,000 people, who have strep throat will get rheumatic fever. Adults can get rheumatic fever, but it usually occurs in children between five and fifteen years of age. We do not know for sure why some children are more susceptible to the fever, but some doctors believe that it may be hereditary, or passed down through the genes from parent to child.

In the United States, rheumatic fever is most common in the northern states and twice as common among women as men. Carson McCullers (1917–1967), an American author (*The Heart Is a Lonely Hunter*, 1940), had several bouts of rheumatic fever as a teenager and fought its complications all her life. If her first attack had been recognized and treated with present-day medicine, she probably would have lived a longer and much healthier life. The 1950s teen idol Bobby Darin (1936–1973) also had rheumatic fever as a child and died at the age of thirty-seven after a singing career that pushed his ailing heart to the limit.

One of the most recognized people who is believed to have had rheumatic fever was the great composer Wolfgang Amadeus Mozart. On November 20, 1791, the thirty-five-year-old Mozart was stricken with a high fever, headaches, a rash, and painful swelling in his arms and legs. He died fifteen days later.

If this list of famous but short-lived rheumatic fever victims seems depressing, remember that all of them got rheumatic fever before effective treatments were

The great composer Wolfgang Amadeus Mozart is believed to have died of rheumatic fever.

available. If they had lived today, they probably would have lived much longer and healthier lives.

What Causes Rheumatic Fever?

Everybody has an immune system. The purpose of the immune system is to fight off infections, and it has many ways of performing this job. One way is to produce special proteins called antibodies, which are designed to fight germs. Though scientists have different theories about the cause of rheumatic fever, and no one theory has been completely proven, evidence suggests that it is a disease in which the human body is attacked by its own immune system.

When you come down with a case of chicken pox, your body is full of the germs that cause the illness. Since you've never had chicken pox before, it takes time for your immune system to make antibodies to fight it. Eventually, with the help of antibodies, your body kills all the chicken pox germs. Even though you might be well, your immune system keeps a few copies of the antibody in case the illness returns. If the chicken pox germs appear again, your body now already has the design for the right antibody from which it can immediately produce many copies. Now your body can destroy the chicken pox germs quickly, well before there are enough of them to make you sick again. If you're attacked again by the germs, chances are you won't even know it.

Even though this is an effective system for the body to fend off disease, it doesn't work perfectly every time. Many scientists believe that the antibodies our immune systems manufacture to fight strep throat bacteria have a way of going wrong—it's possible that they can mistake some parts of our own body for strep throat germs. So, the weapons that are meant to fight off an outside invasion get turned against our own bodies. This, scientists believe, is how a strep throat infection can lead to rheumatic fever.

When Do People Get Rheumatic Fever?

People get rheumatic fever most often during cool, damp weather in the winter and early spring. There is a latent period, a lapse of time that goes by, between the strep infection and the first episode of the fever. This period between the strep infection and the beginning of rheumatic fever can last between one to five weeks, with an average of nineteen days. But an attack can last for three months or longer. About 5 percent of rheumatic fever patients have attacks that last eight months or more. In general, the longer the attack lasts, the worse the damage is. After the attack is over, many people are left with heart damage.

If you have rheumatic fever once, you may have a tendency to get it again. So steps must be taken to prevent another attack. Without those steps, some people may have many attacks of rheumatic fever, and each attack may lead to more heart damage.

What Are the Symptoms of Rheumatic Fever?

Rheumatic fever can easily be mistaken for other diseases. To find out if a patient has rheumatic fever, doctors use a list of symptoms called the Jones criteria, named after T. Duckett Jones, MD, who devised it in 1944. The list has since been revised by the American Heart Association.

The Jones criteria are needed because there is no one symptom, sign, or laboratory test that proves someone has rheumatic fever. Doctors have to diagnose it based on a group of symptoms and the patient's history. If the fever and typical symptoms occur a few weeks after an attack of strep throat, doctors are likely to suspect rheumatic fever.

Not all cases produce all the symptoms. However, some common symptoms are described here.

Polyarthritis

The most noticeable symptom of rheumatic fever is polyarthritis, or pain in the joints. It's called polyarthritis because this type of arthritis, or joint inflammation, affects more than one joint ("poly" means "more than one"). Sometimes it is also called migratory polyarthritis

Arthritis is an illness that causes pain in the joints. Polyarthritis, or pain in more than one joint, is a symptom of rheumatic fever.

because the pain migrates, or moves, throughout the body. That is, it appears first in one or more joints, then in others.

It's also the most common symptom. Up to 70 percent of people with rheumatic fever have arthritis. The pain can be so intense that some children with rheumatic fever have been known to refuse to let bed sheets cover their affected joints. The pain in any one joint usually doesn't last for more than several weeks. The good news is that it usually goes away and does not cause long-term damage.

Carditis

The most serious symptom of rheumatic fever is carditis, an inflammation of the heart. Inflammation can occur in many different parts of the heart including the valves (mitral stenosis or aortic stenosis), the muscles (myocarditis), or the outer covering (pericarditis). If not treated properly, carditis can lead to congestive heart failure, which occurs when the heart fails to pump enough blood to keep up with the needs of the body.

Another reason why carditis is dangerous is because it can cause permanent damage to the heart. About half of the patients with rheumatic fever suffer some degree of lingering heart damage. But even more dangerous is the fact that carditis can go unnoticed by the sufferers and doctors until a great deal of damage has been done. In fact, its signs may not occur until years after the attack of rheumatic fever.

Doctors can tell when a person has carditis because sufferers may have an abnormal heart rhythm. The heart may also beat at a faster-than-normal rate. Doctors can track this with an echocardiogram, a picture of the heart in motion (similar to a live X-ray) produced by a machine that uses high-frequency sound waves.

Sydenham's Chorea

A somewhat rarer symptom of rheumatic fever is Sydenham's chorea, which occurs in about 15 percent of

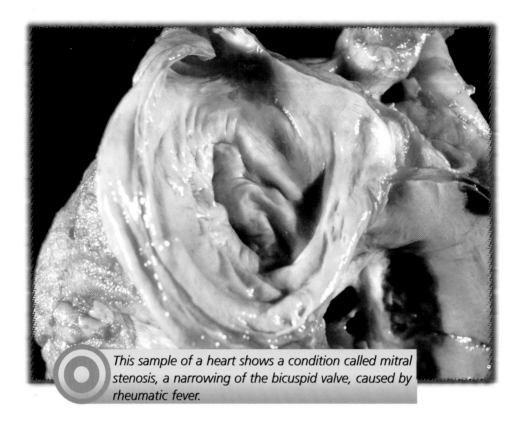

This sample of a heart shows a condition called mitral stenosis, a narrowing of the bicuspid valve, caused by rheumatic fever.

rheumatic fever patients. Sydenham's chorea used to be called Saint Vitus's dance, named after Saint Vitus, the patron saint of dancing. Patients who have Sydenham's chorea make random, sometimes jerky movements they can't control when they're awake. Curiously, the movements usually stop when the patients are asleep. The movements can involve the hands and face. Sometimes they include the tongue, which makes it hard or impossible to understand the patients' speech. Chorea may appear up to three months after the first throat infection. It can also appear after the rheumatic fever attack, often months after other visible symptoms have disappeared. It goes away after a period of weeks or months.

Subcutaneous Nodules

Between 3 and 10 percent of rheumatic fever patients have bumps found mostly over bony areas. These subcutaneous (beneath the skin) nodules tend to disappear in one to two weeks and cause no lasting harm. They're bad signs, though, because they usually appear on patients who have had more than one attack of rheumatic fever. Most rheumatic fever patients who have nodules also have severe heart disease.

Strep Throat and Rheumatic Fever

Group A streptococcus is the bacterium that causes strep throat and sometimes leads to rheumatic fever. But it can cause other illnesses as well, since there are different strains of GAS and because different people can have different reactions to the same bacteria.

Dangerous infections occur when GAS bacteria get into parts of the body where bacteria usually aren't found. GAS in the blood, muscles, or the lungs is called invasive GAS disease. It doesn't occur very often, but when it does, it can be deadly.

One form of invasive GAS disease is a condition called necrotizing fasciitis. In the case of necrotizing

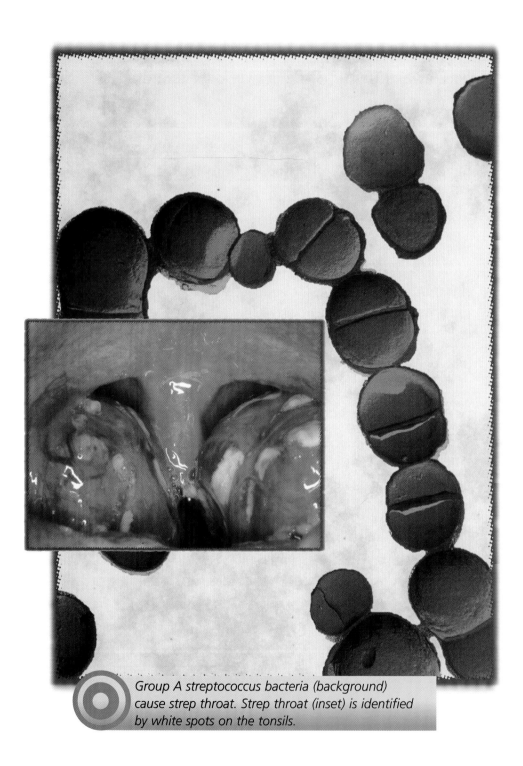

Group A streptococcus bacteria (background) cause strep throat. Strep throat (inset) is identified by white spots on the tonsils.

fasciitis, the bacteria destroy muscles, fat, and skin tissue. Because they destroy so much tissue so rapidly, some newspapers in the early 1990s began calling it the "flesh-eating bacteria." The puppeteer Jim Henson, creator of the Muppets, died in 1990 from an attack of necrotizing fasciitis.

Another form of invasive GAS diseases is streptococcal toxic shock syndrome. Despite occasional scares of an epidemic, both necrotizing fasciitis and streptococcal toxic shock syndrome are rare conditions.

Though all three are caused by the group A streptococcus bacterium, necrotizing fasciitis and streptococcal toxic shock syndrome are completely different illnesses from rheumatic fever.

The Connection

It's taken a long time for doctors to understand why strep throat sometimes leads to rheumatic fever. Even today not everything is known, but doctors now are fairly sure that one reason may be a difference in the bacteria itself. There are many strains of group A streptococcus, and not all of them are associated with rheumatic fever. In fact, most strains probably do not cause it.

Another reason for the connection might be that some people have inherited a susceptibility to rheumatic fever. Their susceptibility is passed down from parent to child even if the parents themselves have never had rheumatic fever. Scientists who study DNA (deoxyribonucleic acid, the genetic blueprint for the body that each of us carries in our cells) have recently found evidence of an inherited susceptibility to rheumatic fever. They have found a genetic marker that is present in 100 percent of rheumatic fever patients, but only in 10 percent of people who have never had rheumatic fever. This strongly suggests that a tendency to get rheumatic fever is inherited. The 10 percent of people with the genetic marker who never get rheumatic fever are probably lucky enough to never be exposed to rheumatic fever–causing bacteria.

A third explanation for the differences between different people's susceptibility to rheumatic fever is the speed with which they get medical attention after strep throat. Right now, this is the factor that is easiest to control.

Chapter 2

A Background

No one knows how long rheumatic fever has been around. But at the end of the eighteenth century, doctors began to notice that children and young adults would sometimes come down with a high temperature and aching joints. Aching joints were usually a problem of the elderly. For young people's joints to ache was unusual, so the doctors began to wonder if they were dealing with a new disease. They called the strange illness acute rheumatism ("acute" means lasting a short time). Victims of acute rheumatism suffered a sudden attack of intense joint pain that eventually went away. It seemed clear that this was different from the rheumatism that so many older people suffered from, which came on gradually and seldom went away for long.

A few doctors also noticed that some of their young patients suffered from chest pains with a few ultimately dying of heart complications. When autopsies were performed, doctors found that the heart valves had been damaged.

Doctors today are pretty certain that these patients suffered from the same rheumatic fever that we know today. Still, there are a lot of differences in early and later descriptions of the disease. Doctors treating acute rheumatism mentioned heart problems much less often than they would in later decades. Sydenham's chorea was only described later. This might have been because the doctors only gradually began to realize that these were all different symptoms of the same disease.

Another explanation is that the symptoms of rheumatic fever changed in nature as time went on, which is possible since bacteria are known to change over the years. When the bacteria change, the diseases they cause can change, too.

Overcrowding and Rheumatic Fever

Fairly early on, doctors noticed that there were more cases of rheumatic fever among the poor than among the middle class and the rich. Poor people tend to be more prone to disease because they generally eat less healthily and cannot afford good medical care.

This tenement from the beginning of the twentieth century is an example of overcrowding, which led to rheumatic fever.

But there was more to the problem than bad nutrition and lack of medical care. Over the years, it has become clear to experts that rheumatic fever occurs more often in overcrowded areas. For example, there are more cases of rheumatic fever in army barracks, where many soldiers live together in a small area, than in the general population. This seems to occur even when the soldiers are well fed and otherwise healthy. It is believed that crowding leads to a higher incidence of the disease by making it easier for the bacteria that cause strep throat—and, consequently, rheumatic fever—to spread. The more close contacts a person has in the course of a day, the greater chance he or she has of catching a germ. This seems to be particularly true of the bacteria that cause strep throat and rheumatic fever.

The link between overcrowding and rheumatic fever may explain why the numbers of people with rheumatic fever increased as the nineteenth century wore on. Before the nineteenth century, most people worked and lived on farms. They seldom traveled very far from their homes. They met only a handful of other people each day, and so had fewer opportunities to spread germs. In England and America in the nineteenth century, however, all this began to change as the use of machinery spread.

Soon, machines were doing more of the work on farms. People moved from farms to cities to find work in factories. Many of them moved to slums where they were packed together in small apartments. When they left their tiny apartments, they went out into city streets that were more crowded than ever before. They lived a city life where, each day, they came into contact with hundreds of strangers. They worked in factories, where they also came into close contact with many more people than ever before. These numerous close contacts made it easier for all kinds of germs to spread.

Even hospitals tended to spread disease among the poor in the nineteenth century. In those days, middle class and wealthy people did not go to hospitals when they were sick—even if they were deathly ill. Instead, doctors visited them in their homes. Hospitals were used largely by poor workers who lived in cities, and the hospitals of the time were not very good. They were crowded and unsanitary. Ironically, the poor caught many diseases from each other in the badly run, unsanitary hospitals of the time.

Slowly Beginning to Understand Rheumatic Fever

As more and more cases of rheumatic fever appeared in hospitals in the big cities of England and America, doctors finally began to see it as a major problem. However, for a long time doctors had no idea what caused the disease, and their ignorance led them to make many mistakes in its treatment and prevention.

It was not until the 1870s that doctors began to realize that germs were a major cause of disease. Even after that, it took a long time for doctors to understand that rheumatic fever was an infectious disease. Since patients usually recover from strep throat before they get rheumatic fever, it was hard to find the bacteria that caused any particular case of rheumatic fever.

Treatments That Didn't Work

Even when doctors were aware of the danger of contagious diseases, they didn't bother to keep rheumatic fever patients away from other patients because they didn't know that it was contagious. Ignorance about the cause and consequences of rheumatic fever also led to useless treatments. We know today that the joint pain that comes with rheumatic fever eventually goes away by itself. But doctors in the nineteenth century concentrated on treating the fever and joint pain and ignored the heart, the most vital organ.

One popular but ineffective treatment for rheumatic fever was the use of alkalis—chemicals that have opposite properties to acids. Acids include such familiar substances as vinegar, the citric acid found in lemon and orange juices, and hydrochloric acid. As you may guess from the list, acids tend to have a sour taste. Alkalis, which are also called bases, include substances like lye and baking soda. They tend to have a bitter taste.

In the 1800s, doctors noticed that many fever patients produced more acid in their sweat and urine than people who were well. Jumping to the conclusion that the disease was related to having too much acid in the body, they treated many of their fever patients with alkaline drugs, which they hoped would neutralize the excess acids. These treatments were of no use.

Meanwhile, more and more children were coming down with the disease.

Doctors Piece Together the Puzzle

Around the beginning of the twentieth century, doctors gradually began to piece together the puzzle. They first realized that rheumatic fever was always preceded by tonsillitis, scarlet fever, or an acute sore throat, which most doctors believed was infectious. Though by 1884 they had already identified and named the streptococcus bacteria, they did not yet know that it caused strep throat and rheumatic fever. There was no "eureka" moment. Instead, through a gradual accumulation of evidence, doctors realized that the bacteria they called group A streptococcus caused strep throat, scarlet fever, and some cases of tonsillitis, and that these infections sometimes led to rheumatic fever. Finally by the 1930s, the ideas of rheumatic fever were essentially the same as those held by doctors today.

The High Tide of Rheumatic Fever

Knowing that strep bacteria caused rheumatic fever didn't help doctors much, though. Medicines that killed bacteria had not yet been developed, so rheumatic fever remained a major public health problem.

How many people had rheumatic fever in the United States when the epidemic was at its worst? We don't know for sure because we don't have records for occurrences of the disease in the United States as a whole. We do know, though, that the problem was very serious. Many large cities maintained entire hospitals just for children with rheumatic fever. Baltimore, Maryland, for example, had the Happy Hills Convalescent Hospital, which opened as a thirty-bed hospital in 1922. By 1929, it had more than doubled in size.

Rheumatic fever continued to be a major scourge of childhood throughout the 1930s and 1940s. Each year, from 1935 to 1949, approximately one out of every 1,500 children between the ages of five and fourteen in Rochester, Minnesota, got the fever. And in the first half of the 1940s, it struck many of the young men who were crowded together in army camps. In some army camps, as many as one out of every 250 people got the disease.

The Decline of Rheumatic Fever

As bad a problem as rheumatic fever was in the 1930s and 1940s, fewer people were getting the disease than in the past. In fact, the incidence of rheumatic fever was declining as early as the late 1920s.

Doctors who study the history of diseases agree that this decline of rheumatic fever occurred. However,

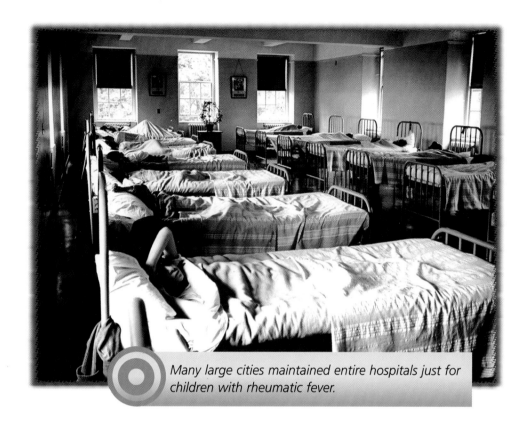

Many large cities maintained entire hospitals just for children with rheumatic fever.

they're far from certain why it occurred. Was it due to advances in medicine? Were doctors getting better at treating rheumatic fever or preventing it by treating strep throat? Probably not, since the medicines that are effective against strep throat did not become widely available until after World War II. By the 1920s and 1930s, doctors had a better understanding of rheumatic fever, but there still wasn't much they could do to prevent or treat it.

The most common explanation for the decline is that general living conditions improved and there was less crowding in the United States. There are still some problems with this explanation, however. The 1930s was the decade of the Great Depression. Times were hard for millions of Americans who were out of work or working for lower wages than they had been in the 1920s. People certainly weren't living better. And cities weren't necessarily less crowded. Some people were even doubling up in small apartments to save on rent money.

Antibiotics

Rheumatic fever started to decline much more sharply in the 1950s and 1960s, and this decline is much easier to explain than previous ones. In 1929, the English scientist Dr. Alexander Fleming made one of the most important discoveries in the history of medicine. Though it is considered one of the most important medical breakthroughs, Fleming's discovery is often described as an accident.

While working in his lab, some bacterial cultures that Fleming was growing in his lab became accidentally contaminated by a type of mold—one of the molds that is present in the air and that we sometimes find growing on food that has been forgotten at the back of the refrigerator. Though he didn't mean for the mold to grow, he realized it was a stroke of luck because this mold had killed all the bacteria that touched it.

Dr. Alexander Fleming discovered penicillin accidentally. It was later used to cure many infectious diseases, including rheumatic fever.

Earlier in his career, Fleming had looked for natural substances that killed bacteria but hadn't found any that worked very well. Looking down at the contaminated petri dish, he realized that he had found what he'd been searching for all this time, a very powerful weapon against bacteria, the germ-killing drug now known as penicillin.

Like many other great discoveries, it took penicillin a long time to make it from the laboratory into everyday life. Many other scientists had to experiment with penicillin before it could become a useful drug. They had to find a way to extract the medicine from the mold and produce it in large quantities. So, even though Fleming made the discovery in 1929, it didn't really begin to make a difference in society until 1943. Once it became widely available, it started to work wonders, saving hundreds of thousands of soldiers in World War II from infections that would have otherwise killed them.

After World War II, penicillin was used to cure many infectious diseases. Among others, it cured strep throat, scarlet fever, and rheumatic fever. Researchers then began to develop other medicines similar to penicillin. Together these drugs form the class of medicines called antibiotics. Without antibiotics, many diseases that were once common would still be serious threats to public health, and rheumatic fever would probably still be the major disease of childhood.

Chapter 3

Living with Rheumatic Fever

Most of the symptoms of rheumatic fever go away. The fever itself, joint pain, rashes, nodules over the swollen joints, and uncontrolled movements of arms, legs, or facial muscles all eventually disappear without causing permanent damage. But carditis—the symptom in which rheumatic fever attacks its victims' hearts—is more serious and more dangerous. This damage, which is usually to the valves of the heart, can be permanent. How serious it is varies greatly from case to case.

Damage to the heart as a result of rheumatic fever is called rheumatic heart disease. The most serious kinds of heart damage that result from rheumatic fever occur when the disease attacks the heart's major valves, the heart muscle, or the heart's outer membrane.

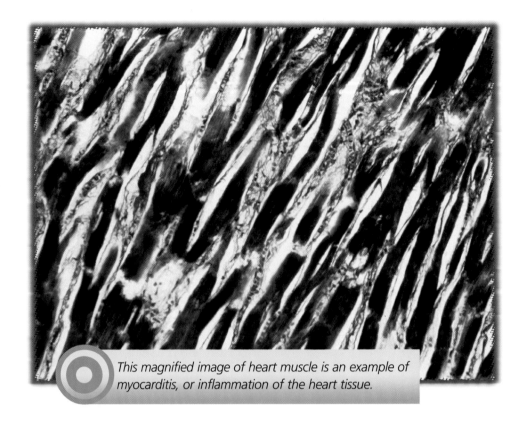

This magnified image of heart muscle is an example of myocarditis, or inflammation of the heart tissue.

Recognizing Rheumatic Heart Disease

Rheumatic heart disease can be helped with treatment, so the most important thing of all is to know if you have it. If you or any member of your family has a bad sore throat that is followed within a few weeks by some of the symptoms of rheumatic fever, a doctor should be consulted immediately. In fact, any long-lasting fever should be reason to see a doctor. Any fever that comes with joint pain should also be a sign to see a doctor.

There is no one simple test for rheumatic fever. Doctors who suspect that you have it will ask questions and take samples of your blood for a number of tests.

Distinguishing Rheumatic Fever from Other Diseases

Many people who have some of the symptoms described in this book may not have rheumatic fever, since it is an illness that is easy to mistake for others. Because of this your doctor should ask questions and conduct tests to figure out what you have. You may have an illness that is just as serious, but which calls for a different treatment, an illness like leukemia or juvenile rheumatoid arthritis. Doctors can make mistakes, so when serious illness is involved it's a good idea to consult more than one doctor.

Treating the Fever

If you do have rheumatic fever, doctors will immediately treat it with anti-inflammatory drugs to help lower the fever and reduce the inflammation. The most well-known anti-inflammatory drug is aspirin, the same drug people have taken for many years to alleviate headaches. However, not all people react well to aspirin. Doctors nowadays use it carefully, watching for bad reactions. If the case seems more severe, doctors may treat the inflammation with drugs called corticosteroids. Corticosteroids are similar to hormones found in the human body and are very successful at reducing inflammation.

Preventing Future Attacks

The most serious health problems caused by rheumatic fever come to people from repeated attacks, so it's very important to take steps to see that your first attack of rheumatic fever is your last. While doctors are reducing the fever and inflammation, they may also start rheumatic fever patients on low doses of antibiotics. Doctors usually recommend that people who have had rheumatic fever keep on taking the antibiotics after the attack is over.

You may need to keep on taking low doses of antibiotics for three to five years after the first episode of rheumatic fever. In some cases, doctors recommend that people who have had rheumatic fever go on taking antibiotics for an even longer time. They may recommend that you continue to take antibiotics until you reach the age of eighteen or even for life, especially if you have had heart damage. Frequent contact with children is another reason to keep on taking antibiotics, as children may be carriers of strep.

Low doses of antibiotics are enough to stop the strep infection from returning and triggering another attack of rheumatic fever. Without these low doses of antibiotics, you may get rheumatic fever again with possible further damage to the heart. With the antibiotics, you can concentrate on getting better.

Assessing the Damage

After immediate treatment for rheumatic fever, tests should be done to assess the damage. This is especially important, because people who suffer from rheumatic heart disease do not always know they have it. The damage may not show up until later in life. Victims of rheumatic fever in childhood have been known to experience heart damage as late as the age of fifty, damage that is a direct result of their initial childhood attack. With treatment, the heart problems caused by rheumatic fever may get better. Left untreated, they may get worse. Even when treatment can't repair damage, it can prevent complications that lead to more damage to the heart and other parts of the body.

Doctors have many ways to find out if a patient has suffered damage to the heart. One of the oldest is simply to listen to the heart using a stethoscope. A heart that has been damaged may have an unusual sound, or a murmur. (Some hearts with murmurs function normally, though, so finding one is not necessarily something to worry about.) Doctors have many other ways of testing for heart damage, particularly the valve damage that is the most common kind of damage caused by rheumatic fever. Most tests, as you'll see below, are not painful and are noninvasive—that is, there's no cutting involved.

Chest X-Ray

A noninvasive step might be a chest X-ray. In a chest X-ray, a small amount of radiation is used to produce a photograph of your insides.

Electrocardiogram

Another test commonly given to check for heart problems is an electrocardiogram. This test takes advantage of the fact that the heart produces electric signals when it beats. In an electrocardiogram, six pieces of metal with wires attached to them are stuck to the surface of your chest, and electric signals produced by the heart make a line graph of the heartbeat. Experts can read the rises and falls of the line and see if there's anything unusual.

Echocardiogram

An even better picture of the heart's functioning in motion is given by an echocardiogram. This procedure

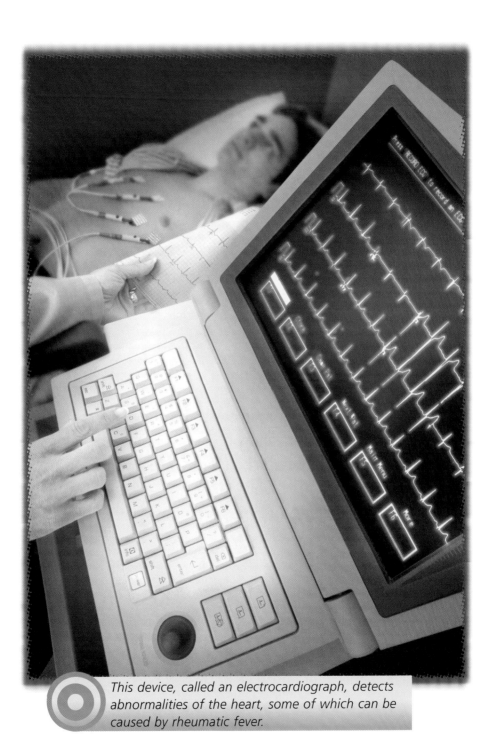

This device, called an electrocardiograph, detects abnormalities of the heart, some of which can be caused by rheumatic fever.

uses high-frequency sound waves to produce an image of the heart and the blood vessels around it.

Doppler Echocardiogram

A related test called a Doppler echocardiogram, or Doppler ultrasound, uses the high-frequency sound waves to show the direction and speed of the blood flow through the heart.

No single one of these tests necessarily tells doctors all they need to know about the way your heart is functioning. But together, they can give an accurate picture of what is happening.

Watch out for Delayed Effects

Some effects of rheumatic fever are delayed, which means they may not show up until years after the attack. So if you've had rheumatic fever, you need to see a doctor regularly. The doctor has to know you've had rheumatic fever and be alert to any signs of the delayed effects.

Damage to the Heart Valves

The most common serious type of heart damage that can be caused by rheumatic fever is damage to the valves of the heart, especially mitral stenosis and aortic stenosis.

Mitral Stenosis

Mitral stenosis is a defect of the valve that separates two chambers of the heart (the left atrium and the left ventricle). It prevents the valve from opening properly and gets in the way of the blood flow from the left atrium to the left ventricle. This blockage can reduce the amount of blood that flows to the body. Sometimes the left atrium enlarges as pressure builds up. And this can cause blood to flow back into the lungs. Mitral stenosis can be a delayed effect of rheumatic fever. If it does not occur at the time of the acute rheumatic fever attack, its symptoms may develop between the ages of twenty and fifty.

People who have mitral stenosis may not realize it until their bodies are stressed, for example by an infection or by pregnancy. Symptoms include trouble breathing (during exercise or when lying flat), cough, blood in the sputum (that is, spit), getting tired easily, frequent respiratory infections, palpitations (feeling your heart beat fast when you're not exercising or excited), swelling of feet or ankles, and in rare cases, chest pain. Most of the symptoms on this list can have other causes, but if you have any of them, you should ask a doctor about them.

Not all cases of mitral stenosis are the same. Thirty percent of the people who get mitral stenosis during or right after they have rheumatic fever show no signs of it a year later. For others, though, it's a lifelong problem. If ignored, it can lead to congestive heart failure, which occurs when the heart is not working well enough to support the body's functions.

Treatment of mitral stenosis varies depending on how severe the case is. The goal of most of the treatment is to prevent the complications of the disease. Some people with mitral stenosis should limit their activities so as not to stress the heart. Every case is different, though. Your doctor will tell you how much exercise is good for you.

Mitral stenosis can lead to blood clots, which can damage the brain and other parts of the body, so people with mitral stenosis often take anticoagulation drugs (drugs that prevent blood clots).

People with mitral stenosis also have a risk of heart infections, so they need to take antibiotics before they undergo any procedure that could let bacteria get into the bloodstream. This includes not only surgery but dental work. Even when you get your teeth cleaned, bacteria can get into your mouth, so antibiotics should be used then, too. In severe cases of mitral stenosis, surgery may be done to repair the damaged valve.

Aortic Stenosis

Aortic stenosis is a somewhat rarer but even more serious consequence of rheumatic heart disease. The aorta is the largest blood vessel in the body, the tube through which oxygen-rich blood is pumped from the right ventricle out to the body. In aortic stenosis, the valve that separates the aorta from the right ventricle becomes narrow. In serious cases, the narrowing interferes with the flow of blood to the body.

Most people who suffer from aortic stenosis have long-term heart disease. They need to take the same precautions taken by people with mitral stenosis. In these serious cases, doctors usually recommend that patients limit their physical activities to avoid putting stress on their hearts.

Chapter 4

Fighting Rheumatic Fever Today

In some parts of the world, especially Asia and Africa, rheumatic fever is still a common disease of childhood. While far fewer people in the United States get rheumatic fever now than in the early twentieth century, it has not been wiped out. It is still the most common acquired heart disease in children and young adults, and it's the main cause of death from heart disease in the first fifty years of life.

Could rheumatic fever come back as a major disease of childhood in the United States? Doctors worry that it might, seeing that the number of cases started to rise in the late 1980s and continued through the 1990s. Though the rise has never reached anything like the numbers found earlier in the twentieth century, it is scary, especially since doctors don't know why it occurred. The outbreaks were concentrated in certain parts of the country, such as Utah and Wyoming. The Primary Children's Medical Center in Salt Lake City recorded a larger number of cases in 1998 than in any of the previous thirty-eight years.

New Strains of Strep?

One worry connected with the rise of rheumatic fever cases is the possibility of a new, harder-to-detect strain of streptococcus bacteria that doesn't produce noticeable symptoms at first, but leads to rheumatic fever. In the late 1990s, scientists looked at the medical records of 478 cases of rheumatic fever treated between 1985 and 1998 at the Primary Children's Medical Center. The records showed that only 20 percent of the patients had sought medical attention for throat problems before coming down with rheumatic fever symptoms. This raised fears about the emergence of a new "stealth" version of the strep bacteria that wouldn't cause a bad sore throat. A strep bacteria that doesn't cause a sore throat could be a big problem because it wouldn't alert people in time to get antibiotics. The existence of such a new strain of strep has not been proven, but the possibility of it remains a concern.

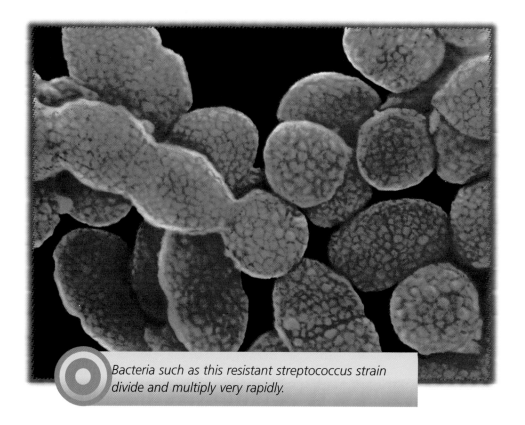

Bacteria such as this resistant streptococcus strain divide and multiply very rapidly.

Another worry—one that extends to many disease-causing bacteria—is the development of strains that antibiotics can't kill. Remember, bacteria evolve just as animals and plants do. When millions of bacteria in a person's body are killed by a particular antibiotic, a few stragglers—the toughest bacteria inside a person's body—may survive. These are the ones that live to multiply. They can pass on their resistance to that particular antibiotic to their descendants.

If this happens often enough, a whole new strain appears that can't be killed by that antibiotic. That's one reason why it's so important to take the full dose of any antibiotic a doctor prescribes. Even after your symptoms disappear, you should keep on taking the medicine until all the bacteria are killed, including any that might be a little tougher and more antibiotic-resistant than the others. Saving some for later is always a mistake.

To prevent new strains of antibiotic-resistant bacteria from appearing, public health authorities also caution doctors against overusing antibiotics—that is, using them for infections that aren't serious enough to require them. It would be a tragedy for modern medicine to lose its most powerful weapon against infection.

Strep Vaccines

In the 1970s, a few companies went to work developing a vaccine for strep throat. A strep vaccine could be very popular. Not only would it prevent rheumatic fever, it would prevent other serious conditions. It would also prevent many less serious but painful sore throats.

However, since rheumatic fever is probably an overreaction of the immune system to strep bacteria, developing a vaccine for it is tricky. A strep vaccine needs to teach the body to be reactive enough to hit strep hard as soon as it appears, but not so reactive as to attack itself.

That may have been the problem with the research done in the 1970s. In 1979, one of the experimental strep vaccines seemed to trigger a case of rheumatic fever. The Food and Drug Administration (FDA) banned the human use of products containing group A streptococcus, including vaccines containing them. Companies quit spending their own money to develop vaccines against strep. Research continued at a slower pace with money provided by the National Institutes of Health.

Since then, the FDA hasn't officially changed its mind, but the rise in rheumatic fever cases has made the search for a vaccine more urgent, and scientific advances have made vaccine development safer. The FDA let two companies, Siga in New York and ID Biomedical in Vancouver, British Columbia, begin early-stage testing in adults in 2002. It will take years of testing to prove that these vaccines are safe and effective. If and when they do, the FDA is expected to lift its ban on strep vaccines.

Genetic Markers

In another promising area of research, doctors will soon be able to predict who would be susceptible to rheumatic fever. Now that the genetic marker for rheumatic fever has been found, tests can be created that will show which people are at risk for the disease. These are the people who should be given a vaccine

Vaccinations prevent infection and the spread of many diseases.

against strep, once a safe and effective vaccine has been developed.

Even without advanced genetic techniques, you may be able to guess if you are at risk for rheumatic fever simply by looking at your family history. If other members of your family have had rheumatic fever, whether now or a generation or two back, you should consider yourself at risk. You should be especially alert to the symptoms of strep infections and see a doctor promptly when you have a sore throat.

Glossary

antibiotics Substances produced by microbes that can harm or kill other microbes.

antibodies Proteins produced by the immune system to fight disease.

aortic stenosis Deformation of the valve between the right ventricle of the heart and the aorta.

bacteria Extremely small one-celled organisms that usually have a cell wall and multiply by cell division.

carditis Inflammation of the heart.

echocardiogram A procedure that generates a moving picture of the heart.

electrocardiogram A diagnostic procedure that detects electric signals produced by the heart.

deoxyribonucleic acid (DNA) The molecule that is found in the cells of every living creature and which contains the plan or "blueprint" for the body.

group A streptococcus (GAS) A group of bacteria responsible for many infectious diseases, including step throat, scarlet fever, and rheumatic fever.

immune system The body's system that has the task of fighting off infection.

mitral stenosis Deformation of the valve between the left atrium and left ventricle of the heart.

myocarditis Inflammation of the heart muscle.

penicillin The first antibiotic discovered, and still the preferred treatment against group A streptococcus.

polyarthritis Arthritis in more than one kind of joint.

rheumatic fever A fever accompanied by inflammation of many of the body's tissues, which occurs as a delayed consequence of a strep throat infection.

rheumatism Painful inflammation of the joints or muscles.

subcutaneous nodules Bumps under the skin, a symptom of rheumatic fever.

Sydenham's chorea Random, uncontrollable body movements associated with temporary nerve damage due to rheumatic fever.

vaccine A medication designed to stimulate the body's immune system to generate a response that will protect the individual from disease. Each vaccine stimulates a response to a particular infectious agent.

Where to Go for Help

American Heart Association
7272 Greenville Avenue
Dallas, TX 75231
(800) 242-8721
Web site: http://www.americanheart.org

Centers for Disease Control and Prevention (CDC)
1600 Clifton Road
Atlanta, GA 30333
(404) 639-3311
Web site: http://www.cdc.gov

National Heart, Lung and Blood Institute
P.O. Box 30105
Bethesda, MD 20824-0105
(301) 592-8573
Web site: http://www.nhlbi.nih.gov

National Institute of Allergy and
      Infectious Diseases
Building 31, Room 7A-50
31 Center Drive MSC 2520
Bethesda, MD 20892-2520
Web site: http://www.niaid.nih.gov

World Health Organization
525 23rd Street NW
Washington, DC 20037
(202) 974-3000
e-mail: postmaster@paho.org
Web site: http://www.who.int

Web Sites

Due to the changing nature of Internet links, the
Rosen Publishing Group, Inc., has developed an online
list of Web sites related to the subject of this book.
This site is updated regularly. Please use this link to
access the list:

http://www.rosenlinks.com/ntk/rufe

For Further Reading

Avraham, Regina. *Circulatory System.* New York: Chelsea House Publishers, 1999.

Farrell, Jeanette. *Invisible Enemies: Stories of Infectious Disease.* New York: Farrar, Straus & Giroux, 1998.

Johansson, Philip. *Heart Disease.* New York: Enslow Publishers, Inc., 1998.

Massell, Benedict F. *Rheumatic Fever and Streptococcal Infection: Unraveling the Mysteries of a Dread Disease.* Cambridge, MA: Harvard University Press, 1997.

Neill, Catherine A., Edward B. Clark, and Carleen Clark. *The Heart of a Child: What Families Need to Know About Heart Disorders in Children*, 2nd ed. Baltimore: Johns Hopkins University Press, 2001.

Parker, Steve. *Human Body* (Eyewitness Books). New York: DK Publishing, 1999.

Stille, Darlene R. *The Circulatory System* (True Books). New York: Children's Press, 1998.

Taranta, Angelo V., and Milton Markowitz. *Rheumatic Fever.* New York: Kluwer Academic Publishers, 1990.

Bibliography

English, Peter C. *Rheumatic Fever in America and Britain: A Biological, Epidemiological, and Medical History.* Piscataway, NJ: Rutgers University Press, 1999.

Massell, Benedict F. *Rheumatic Fever and Streptococcal Infection: Unraveling the Mysteries of a Dread Disease.* Cambridge, MA: Harvard University Press, 1997.

Markowitz, Milton, and Leon Gordis. *Rheumatic Fever.* Philadelphia: W. B. Saunders, 1972.

Stollerman, Gene H. *Rheumatic Fever and Streptococcal Infection.* New York: Grune & Stratton, 1975.

Taranta, Angelo V., and Milton Markowitz *Rheumatic Fever.* New York: Kluwer Academic Publishers, 1989.

Index

About the Author

Phillip Margulies is a freelance writer living and working in New York City.

Photo Credits

Cover, p. 22 © Custom Medical Stock Photo; pp. 2, 33 © Hansel Mieth/Time Life Pictures/Getty Images, Inc.; p. 7 © Ed Bock/Corbis; p. 14 © Archivo Iconografico, S.A./Corbis; p. 18 © Tom and Dee Ann McCarthy/Corbis; p. 20 © CNRI/Science Photo Library; p. 27 © Bettmann/Corbis; p. 35 © Hulton/Archive/Getty Images; p. 38 © Astrid & Hanns Frieder Michler/Science Photo Library; p. 43 © Lester Lefkowitz/ Corbis; p. 50 © Dr. Kari Lounatmaa/Science Photo Library; p. 53 © Jose Luis Pelaez/Corbis.

Designer: Thomas Forget; Editor: Nicholas Croce